cd9. (and 99 other coded texts they use)

by zoë baloo

For my kids- You
know who
 you are, thanks
for always
keeping
me on my toes.

CD9 or 9
"a parent is watching"

1. **tea** – hot gossip.
   "come on, girl...
   spill the tea!"

2. **yeet** – to throw
something very
hard or fast
          " i'll yeet
your phone if you
say that again"

3. **yaass** – an enthusiastic way of saying "yes."

4. **bruh** – same as "bro."

5. **suh or sup** – a shortened version of "what's up?"

6. **salty** – the way someone acts when they're upset.

7. **tbh** – acronym for "to be honest."

8. **kiki** – to celebrate or share gossip.

9. **basic** – something or someone mainstream, popular and trendy.

10. **swole** – used to describe someone who is physically fit, muscular or works out.

11. **irl**– acronym for "in real life."

12. **ghost** – when a guy or girl is suddenly gone without saying anything. they went "ghost."

13. humble brag –
when someone
complains about
their life while
subtly bragging.

14. **cray or cray cray** – Crazy.

15. **tfw** – acronym for "that feeling when" or "that face when."

16. **bounce** – leaving suddenly.

17. smh – acronym for "shaking my head."

18. **phubbing** – snubbing someone by ignoring them and paying attention to your phone instead.

19. **dead or ded**

– something totally hysterical. "did you watch that Netflix show last night? I'm totally dead!"

20. **low-key**
– something you really (secretly) want. "i want to go to the movies with tonya, but low-key I'd much rather chill out tonight."

21. **high-key**
– straight up the truth.

25

22. **ship** – short for "relationship."

23. mom – The most responsible friend (or "mom") in the group.

24. hundo p – term used when you are 100% sure or certain.

25. **lit** – something that's "awesome or cool," or could also mean "drunk, stoned, high." "my friends and I got so lit last night!"

26. **fomo** – acronym for "fear of missing out."

27. **jomo–** acronym for "joy of missing out."

28. **kk** – okay, gotcha, message received.

29. **squad** – a close friend group.

30. **g.o.a.t.**
– acronym for
"greatest of all time."

31. **savage** – a cooler way to say "cool" or could mean "badass" or "harsh."

"my friend was savage when he walked out of class."

32. **woke** – aware of and actively attentive to facts and issues.

33. damn, gina! – a way to express approval or what you'd say to someone who looks amazing.

34. **keep it 100** – Be real and authentic, not fake.

35. **snatched**
– when someone looks good, perfect or fashionable. "girl, your outfit is snatched."

36. **im weak** – when you laugh so hard you become weak.

37. **goals** – a subtle way to say that you're jealous, something you want or a place you'd like to be.

38. **gucci**
– Something that is good, cool or fine.

39. fam – closest friends are "fam" or like family.

40. **receipts** – show me the proof or "receipts."

41. **extra** – someone who is acting over the top or dramatic.

45

42. beat or beat my face – to apply makeup well or put a lot on.

43. **on fleek** – used to describe someone who
is fashionable or could mean "on point." That girl has some
 serious dance moves that are on fleek!"

44. **slay** – when someone did something amazingly well or looks amazing.

45. clap back – a comeback with attitude.

46. **dank** – very good, excellent, or cool. can also be used to describe something, usually marijuana.

47. **bae** – same as "baby" or "sweetheart." bae is an acronym for "before anyone else."

48. **fire** – something that's really good, hot or trendy.

49. **don't trip**
– don't worry or stress out.

50. **mood** – used to express something that is relatable. similar to or "same."

51. **boujee**
– someone who is rich or is acting rich or fancy.

52. **thicc** – someone (typically a fuller figure) who is sexy and curvy.

53. **sic or sick**
– something that is cool.

54. **creeper**
– someone who is socially awkward or has stalker tendencies.

55. **no cap** – means "no lie," or "im not lying."

56. **straight fire**
– something that is hot or trendy.

57. **finna** – same
ad "going to" or
"about to".

58. **hangry** – a combination of hungry and angry. "you need to eat something girl, youre acting hangry".

59. **sus** – someone who is shady, suspicious or not to be trusted.

"youre sus bro"

60. **tight** – when a couple is in a tight relationship or something is really good.

"thats tight"

61. **shook** – utter disbelief, shocked or surprised. "im shook"

62. **v** – short for "very."

63. skrrt – meant to mimic the sound of screeching tires or to leave.

64. **throw shade**
– to put someone down or comment negatively toward them.

65. **swerve** – to dodge someone or a situation.

66. **af** – acronym for "as f#ck."

67. **thirsty** – used to describe someone who is eager or desperate; horny.

68. **thirst trap** – a sexy photo or flirtatious message posted on social media.

69. **crashy**
– someone who is crazy and trashy.

73

70. **jelly** – jealous.

71. **catfishing**
– pretending to be someone else on social media.

72. **ratchet** – used to describe someone who
 is obnoxious, rude or trashy. "shes ratchet".

73. **bb–** short for babe or baby.

74. **netflix n' chill**
– A way of inviting someone over with the intention of hooking up or having sex.

75. **420**

– marijuana. (april 20th is national weed day.)

79

76. **smash** – casual sex.

77. **tool** – someone who is stupid or is an ass.

78. **pos** – acronym for "parent over shoulder" when texting or "piece of sh#t."

79. **nifoc** – acronym for "naked in front of the computer."

80. **cu46** – see you for sex.

81. **molly** – mdma – a dangerous party drug

82. **snack** – a way to describe someone who looks good or "tasty."

83. **turnt up**
– partying to the max by getting drunk or high. Can also describe general excitement or craziness.

84. **zip ghost**
– someone who is high on marijuana and who isn't functioning well.

85. **53x** – sex.

86. **pron** – porn.

87. **crunk** – getting drunk and high at the same time.

88. bye, felicia – a nasty term used when you want to dismiss someone.

89. **trolls** – someone who purposely tries to provoke others.

90. **bet** – a response that indicates agreement. "youll be there, right?" "bet".

91. body count – the number of people someone has slept with.

92. **finsta**– fake instagram account.

93. **plug** – term used to describe someone who can "connect" you with drugs; a drug dealer.

94. **bih** – short for "b#tch."

95. **fwb** – friends with benefits.

96. **yolo** – meaning, "you only live once."

97. **cap** – fake or lie.

98. **ceebs** – (pronounced "seebs") meaning "total lack of interest."

99. hits different – when something is better than it normally is because of different circumstances.

"this book just hits different"

lastly....

troll: someone that baits people
  to provoke or cause
an emotional
reaction.
          "dad, you're
the biggest troll i
know"